the Garfield Gallery 3

Jim Davis

RAVETTE BOOKS

First published by Ravette Books Limited 1992

Printed and bound for Ravette Books Limited
3 Glenside Estate, Star Road,
Partridge Green, Nr. Horsham,
West Sussex RH13 8RA
An Egmont Company
by STIGE, Italy

ISBN 1 85304 396 6

If you want to look thinner... hang around people fatter than you

JIM DAVIS

JIM DAVIS

GARFIELD EATING TIPS

1. Never eat anything that's on fire.

2. Never leave your food dish under a bird cage.

3. Only play in your food if you've already eaten your toys.

4. Eat every meal as though it were your last.

5. Only snack between meals.

6. Chew your food at least once.

7. Avoid fruits and nuts: after all, you are what you eat.

8. Always dress up your leftovers: one clever way is with top hats and canes.

9. A handy breakfast tip: always check your Grape Nuts for squirrels.

10. Don't save your dessert for last. Eat it first.

be your own
best friend

JIM DAVIS

GARFIELD: © 1978 United Feature Syndicate, Inc.

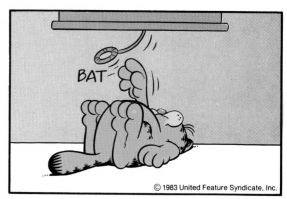

Being a superstar isn't a pretty job but someone has to do it

JiM DAViS

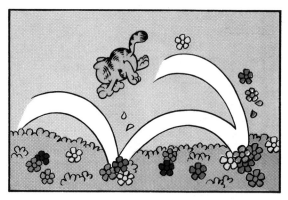

TEDDY BEARS. They don't eat your food, dance with your date, or trump your ace lead.

JIM DAVIS

This business of sleeping holds a great deal of fascination for me

JIM DAVIS

© 1982 United Feature Syndicate, Inc.

Remember... Today is the first day of the rest of your life

JIM DAViS

Here's to weekends

MY ADDRESS HAS CHANGED

Having a wonderful time!

LAST ONE IN'S A ROTTEN EGG!

YOU FIRST, POOKY

BACK FLIP!